LIFE INSIDE THE
MERCHANT MARINE ACADEMY

MAGDALENA ALAGNA

HIGH
interest
books

Children's Press®
A Division of Scholastic Inc.
New York/Toronto/London/Auckland/Sydney
Mexico City/New Delhi/Hong Kong

Book Design: Daniel Hosek
Contributing Editor: Scott Waldman

Dedicated to Sam Stout and Nicolas Fenzel

Photo Credits: Cover, pp. 9, 13, 21, 22, 25, 27, 29, 31, 37 © Michael S. Yamashita/
Corbis; p. 5 © Stephanie Maze/Corbis; p. 6 © Kelly-Mooney Photography/Corbis;
pp. 10, 18, 34 courtesy of Defense Visual Information Center, March ARB, California;
p. 11 © Corbis; p. 14 © Dennis Degnan/Corbis; p. 17 © Adam Woolfitt/Corbis; p. 19
© Ed Kashi/Corbis; p. 33 © Paul A. Souders/Corbis; p. 35 © José F. Poblete; p. 38
© Wolfgang Kaehler/Corbis; p. 40 © Yogi, Inc./Corbis

Library of Congress Cataloging-in-Publication Data

Alagna, Magdalena.
Life inside the Merchant Marine Academy / by Magdalena Alagna.
    p. cm.—(Insider's look)
Includes index.
Summary: Explores the challenges and rewards of attending the United
States Merchant Marine Academy in King's Point, New York, where
individuals are trained to become Merchant Marine officers.
ISBN 0-516-23923-6 (lib. bdg.)—ISBN 0-516-24003-X (pbk.)
1. United States Merchant Marine Academy—Juvenile literature. [1.
United States Merchant Marine Academy. 2. Occupations.] I. Title. II.
Series.
VK525.U6 A8 2002
387.5'071'1747245--dc21

                                                                2002001900

CONTENTS

Introduction

Have you ever thought about traveling all around the world? Have you ever wanted to serve your country? Do you want to get a free college education? If so, then maybe the United States Merchant Marine Academy (USMMA) is for you. The USMMA was founded in 1943. Since then, it has been giving students a challenging education as well as job training. At the USMMA, who you are, and who you become, are just as important as the kind of job for which you are studying. The academy provides an education that will challenge your mind, your body, and your personality.

The Merchant Marines operate many of the large commercial ships in the United States. These ships include cargo ships, passenger

ships, and tankers. The Merchant Marines are in charge of transporting people, raw materials, and manufactured goods to places all over the world. At the USMMA, students are trained for a wide variety of jobs in the maritime industry.

While at the USMMA, you will spend a year at sea. This time is broken up into two six-month periods. At sea, you'll learn about the many different jobs that keep a ship in good working order. At the academy, there's plenty to do even when you're not studying. You can join one of the sports teams, such as the lacrosse team, or get involved in other activities, such as the drama club. The academy has something for everyone! There's even a career placement office to help you get a job when you graduate from the academy. The best part about the USMMA is that the tuition is free. The government will pay for your entire education. However, when you graduate you will have a commitment to both the maritime industry as well as the U.S. Naval Reserve.

How do you get into the USMMA? What will you study there? How is the USMMA different than a civilian college or university? How long is the commitment to the maritime industry and the naval reserves? Read on to find out the answers to these questions and more.

CHAPTER ONE

The History of the Academy

The U.S. government started to train people to work on ships as early as 1874. In 1934, there was a terrible fire aboard the passenger ship *Morro Castle*. Many people died. If the crew of the *Morro Castle* had been better prepared, lives may have been saved. The U.S. Congress realized that people working on ships needed special training. In 1938, the U.S. Merchant Marine Cadet Corps was founded. Training was held at temporary places until the United States Merchant Marine Academy's buildings were finished and ready to be used. In 1943, the USMMA opened at its present location in Kings Point, New York. When President Franklin D. Roosevelt dedicated the academy

The USMMA campus is located in Kings Point, New York, on Long Island. It is about 20 miles east of New York City.

on September 30, 1943, he said, "The academy serves the Merchant Marines as West Point serves the army and Annapolis the navy."

During World War II, USMMA students had their usual course of study interrupted. They went to work as emergency Merchant Marine officers. The academy trained these officers in just twenty-four months! Usually, students take four years to graduate from the USMMA. In World War II, the academy proved that it could train people to serve their country. In time, the academy also proved that it could provide a great education. In 1949, Congress gave the USMMA the right to give out degrees.

ACADEMY FACTS
The USMMA has trained important military professionals who served in the Korean and Vietnam Wars. Graduates have also been sent to the conflicts in the Persian Gulf in 1991 and more recently, to Operation Restore Hope in Somalia from 1992 to 1993.

In 1991, USMMA graduates traveled on these ships to the Persian Gulf.

CHAPTER TWO

Choosing the USMMA

Why should you choose the USMMA over a civilian college or university? What makes the USMMA different? One big difference is that the USMMA trains you for a specific career. Some USMMA students even find jobs before they graduate. Also, at the USMMA, extracurricular activities, such as sailing, can help train you for your career. If you want a career working on or around big ships, it might be a good idea to go to a school where you'll get plenty of chances to learn all about ships and sailing. At the USMMA, you'll get plenty of hands-on experience.

Each year, about 270 men and women are accepted to be the plebe, or first year, class. The USMMA requires its students to be of good

USSMA students who are on a sailing team take part in races, such as this one in Long Island Sound in New York.

Basketball is one of the many sports offered by
the USMMA.

moral character. Applicants must be at least seventeen years old, but not older than twenty-five, on July 1 of the year they are admitted to the school. They must also be citizens of the United States. Potential students have to meet the same physical requirements of a U.S. Naval Reserve midshipman. Midshipmen are students at a naval academy.

The admissions committee reviews an applicant's high school record, Scholastic Aptitude Test (SAT) or American College Test (ACT) scores, recommendations from teachers, and any extracurricular activities he or she may have done. It is a good idea to apply early because the application process is a long one. For more details or to apply on-line, visit the *www.usmma.edu* Web site.

ACADEMIC REQUIREMENTS

You must have a high school diploma or a General Educational Development (GED) certificate that shows you've taken at least fifteen academic credits. You need at least four of those credits in English and three in mathematics (algebra, geometry, and trigonometry). You also need one credit in physics or chemistry, with a laboratory class. That's the least you need to get in. It is a good idea to take four years of mathematics and to take both physics and chemistry.

Courses in mechanical drawing and machine shop are also recommended. Also, you must graduate in the top 40 percent of your high school class if you want a good chance of getting nominated to the academy.

THE NOMINATION

A nomination is when somebody supports your application for admission to the academy. To be considered for admission to the USMMA, you need to be nominated by a congressperson or senate representative. This person may have his or her own requirements for nominating an applicant. Sometimes these requirements include a screening exam. The best time to apply for a nomination is in May of your

TO APPLY FOR THE USMMA

- Request an application from your school guidance counselor or from the USMMA.
- Request a nomination by writing to your state representative.
- Take the SAT or the ACT no later than the first test date of the year for which you're applying.
- Pass a physical exam at a doctor's office.
- Complete the application and return it to the academy with your high school transcripts and letters of recommendation.
- The application must be received by the USMMA no later than March 1 of the year you wish to enter the academy.

One of the most important steps in completing a
USMMA application is getting a recommendation
from your state representative.

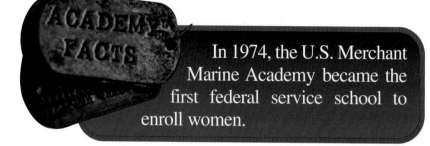

ACADEMY FACTS

In 1974, the U.S. Merchant Marine Academy became the first federal service school to enroll women.

junior year of high school. You request a nomination as a candidate for the academy by writing a letter to a congressperson or senate representative from your state.

CADETS MOVING FORWARD

There are many ways in which a degree from the USMMA will serve you. First, you will have many job opportunities. Graduates have gone on to be astronauts in the National Aeronautic Space Administration (NASA) programs. Others have been ensigns with the U.S. Coast Guard, aviators in the air force, attorneys specializing in military law, and more. Secondly, when you graduate, you'll be an ensign in the Merchant Marine Reserve, which is a part of the U.S. Naval Reserve. You must be a part of the naval reserve for eight years. How you choose to spend those years is up to you. Career opportunities in the U.S. armed forces are very broad. The naval reserve needs doctors, lawyers, social workers, accountants, chefs, physical therapists, as well as professionals for many other positions. The choice is yours to make.

USMMA offers one full year of training on a ship at sea. In fact, it is the only college that offers that amount of training time. At the USMMA, you will do more than just study from books. You will also be trained to work onshore. You will learn everything you need to know to be a Merchant Marine officer.

CHAPTER THREE

Studying at the USMMA

When you first arrive at the academy you will go through a process called indoctrination. Indoctrination lasts for two weeks and prepares you for life at the USMMA. During these two weeks you will receive military training and be challenged physically. Regular classes start after indoctrination. During the beginning of your plebe year, you will take the basic courses you need to graduate. You take courses in the major you choose during the last part of your plebe year.

During the plebe year, you will take courses that you will find at any college. They include chemistry, physics, calculus, computer science, English, history, and physical education. You will also take some courses that you won't find

at a regular college. These courses will be in naval science and ship's medicine.

The major you choose will depend on the kind of merchant marine license you want to receive. The seven majors that you can choose from are:

These USMMA students are learning how to read maps on board a large ship.

1. The marine transportation program prepares you to be a deck officer on a merchant ship. This is a good major to choose if you are interested in business management, either at sea or onshore.

2. The maritime operations and technology program is a great choice if you are interested in both marine transportation and marine engineering. You will learn how to command today's ships.

3. The logistics and intermodal transportation program teaches you to design, operate, and maintain transportation systems. You should pick this major if you are interested in global shipping and transportation.

If you choose a major in one of the three marine transportation programs described on this page, you can work:
- As a deck officer on a merchant ship
- In port and in terminal operations and administration
- In intermodal transportation systems, such as rail, truck, and ship transport systems
- In ship brokerage and chartering
- In maritime sales and marketing
- In admiralty and business law
- In state and federal agencies that regulate transportation and commerce
- As an armed forces officer

4. In the marine engineering program, you will serve as an engineering officer at sea or on land. When you graduate, you will take an exam to be a third assistant engineering officer.

5. The marine engineering systems program teaches you more about the theory of engineering. You can specialize in engineering design. When you graduate, you will be ready to take the exam to be a third assistant engineer.

6. The marine engineering and shipyard management program is for those who want to learn about shipbuilding, ship repair and maintenance, and ship operations. This major is also for those who want a management position.

If you choose a major in one of the three marine engineering programs described on this page, you can work:
- As an engineering officer on a merchant ship
- In naval architecture
- In ship construction and repair
- In equipment design, sales, and maintenance
- In hull and boiler surveying
- In port and terminal operations and administration
- In admiralty law
- In local, state, and federal government regulatory agencies
- In research
- As an armed forces officer

These USMMA students are practicing repairing engines at the Diesel Lab at the academy.

7. There is a dual license program for students interested in earning two licenses. One license is for marine engineering and the other for marine transportation. People in this program will have job opportunities in the marine transportation and marine engineering programs.

THE SEA YEAR

Sea Year covers parts of your sophomore and junior years. You will go to sea twice during your time at the USMMA. Each time at sea lasts about six months, and you will be aboard a commercial or a military ship. You finish with a two- to six-week internship at an onshore maritime or a transportation business.

After Sea Year, you finish the academic program. Before graduation, you must take an exam to get your license to be a Merchant Marine officer. You must also choose your commission in the U.S. Naval Reserve or another uniformed service. This is to meet the military commitment that you made.

CHAPTER FOUR

Life at the USMMA

USMMA students wake up at 6:00 A.M. when the bugle plays reveille. They wash up, get dressed, and clean their rooms, then eat breakfast. Classes are from 8:00 A.M. to 4:00 P.M., with a break for lunch. There are a couple of hours of free time before dinner. Many students choose to participate in extracurricular activities during this time. Evening hours are used for study time. The students' day ends at 11:20 P.M. when the bugle plays taps and the lights are turned off.

CLUBS

Life at the USMMA isn't all work. There are plenty of sports, clubs, and activities to choose from. Whatever your interest is, from photography to karate, you can find a club for it at the USMMA.

Before mealtime, USMMA students yell chants in the mess hall.

There is a school band, a glee club, and a choir for those with musical interests. There are also small bands that perform dance, rock, and jazz music.

If you like to write, you can join *Hear This*, the student newspaper. You can also help to put together the yearbook, or be a part of the debate team. There are a lot of clubs for people interested in engineering, too. These include the Society of Naval Architects and Engineers, the Marine Technology Society, and the Society of Women Engineers.

ATHLETICS

If you like sports, you can join a varsity sports team. You can choose from eighteen different sports, including baseball, basketball, crew, cross-country, golf, rifle, tennis, soccer, swimming, lacrosse, football, volleyball, water polo, and wrestling. Of course, you also have the opportunity to do plenty of sailing.

There are ten varsity athletic teams for women at the USMMA. One of the most popular teams is the softball team. All varsity teams compete against teams from other colleges and universities. In the past, some of the colleges that USMMA played against included Drew University, Brooklyn College, and the U.S. Coast Guard Academy.

Football is one of the team sports that gets a lot of attention at the academy.

There are also intramural sports competitions at the USMMA. Intramural sports are those in which the players on both teams are USMMA students. These include sports such as bowling, softball, and swimming. Touch football, volleyball, soccer, wrestling, and racquetball are also popular. There are club sports in martial arts and rugby, too.

BOATING, CREW, AND OTHER WATER SPORTS

Chances are you're interested in water sports if you are interested in attending the USMMA. The USMMA has plenty of activities that are water related. For instance, there is the crew team. Crew is a racing sport in which teams row boats. In crew sports, you'll combine your love of being on the water with the teamwork and the competitive spirit that can give you a successful edge.

There are other chances to sail besides being a part of a crew team. There is an offshore sailing team that goes to Bermuda to compete. The USMMA also competes in sailing events against other colleges. There is even a power squadron, which commands larger ships, such as whalers and cruising sailboats.

Crew is a popular sport at the USMMA. Most crew athletes lift weights to stay in top shape.

You can also be a part of the windsurfing club. Although the windsurfing club does race, the main purpose of the club is to have a good time on the water. The club holds barbecues and other social events in which you can get to know people with the same interest in sailing that you have.

LEAVING CAMPUS

Students at the USMMA go to lectures, plays, and concerts that are held on campus. However, they may also attend such events elsewhere. Nearby New York City has museums, Broadway and Off-Broadway plays, and plenty of live music to enjoy. Areas of New York, such as the East Village and Chinatown, have many great restaurants.

ACADEMY FACTS

What do you think *Blue Thunder*, *Growler*, and *Maverick* mean at the USMMA? They are the names of some of the boats on the power squadron.

CHAPTER FIVE

After You Graduate

THE SERVICE OBLIGATION

The service obligation is one of the important parts of your education at the USMMA. When you graduate from the academy, you must serve in both the maritime industry and the naval reserve. You become enlisted in the reserves during a ceremony in your plebe year. It is called Acceptance Day. On that day, you pledge to serve in the naval reserve.

When you start at the academy, you sign an agreement. There are several parts to this agreement. First, you agree to graduate from the USMMA. Then, you agree to become a licensed officer in the Merchant Marines. You are also required to apply to be a commissioned officer in the reserve part of the armed forces.

This bell is rung every year at the Acceptance Day ceremonies.

USMMA graduates often work on Coast Guard cutters, such as this one, off the coast of Newfoundland, Canada.

This includes the U.S. Naval Reserve and the U.S. Coast Guard Reserve. You will have to serve in one of the armed forces reserves for eight years.

You must also work in the maritime industry for five years after graduation. The job you choose must have the approval of the U.S. Maritime Administration. Such jobs include any of the jobs that were discussed in chapter three. You can be a commissioned officer on active duty in one of the U.S. armed forces. You can also work for the National Oceanic and Atmospheric Administration.

So, how will these obligations and agreements affect your career choices? Will you have to put your career on hold while you're fulfilling your service obligations? The answer to that question is no. You can do many of the same jobs in the armed forces that you can do in the civilian world.

YOUR SAILING CAREER

When you graduate from the USMMA, you can sail as a licensed third mate or as a third assistant engineer. A third mate works on the bridge of a ship. The bridge is the part of a ship from which the ship is navigated. A third mate makes sure that the ship is safe and that it can safely get to where it's going. Once the

People who work in the engine room of a large ship

ship is in port, a third mate makes sure that the cargo on the ship is loaded and unloaded properly. A third assistant engineer works in the engine or control room. He or she watches out for the ship's power plant. The third assistant engineer helps to keep the ship's machinery and all of its systems in good working order.

You can choose to work on a ship involved in deep-sea foreign or domestic trade. This is a great way to see the world, as you'll often travel to foreign countries. There are also ships that sail domestic waterways, such as the Great Lakes. Or, you could work on a ship that's doing offshore drilling. You could work in a fleet that is owned by or chartered to the U.S. Navy's Military Sealift Command. When you start your career at the USMMA the possibilities are practically unlimited!

WHEN YOU GRADUATE FROM THE USMMA, YOU WILL HAVE:

- A bachelor of science degree
- A license as a Merchant Marine officer
- A commission as ensign in the U.S. Naval Reserve or an active-duty commission in one of the other armed forces

NEW WORDS

cargo things that are on a ship

civilian someone who is not a part of one of the military armed forces

ensign the most junior rank of officer

extracurricular not part of the regular program of study

intermodal many ways of transportation, such as railways, trucks, and ships

intramural having to do with competing teams within one's own school

maritime having to do with the sea or with sailing ships

NEW WORDS

merchant ship a ship that transports cargo that is bought, sold, or traded

midshipman a student in a naval academy

reserves those members of the armed forces that are not on active duty

reveille a piece of music used as a morning wake-up call

varsity the senior branch of athletics in a school

FOR FURTHER READING

Heitzman, Wm. Ray. *Marine and Maritime Careers.* Lincolnwood, IL: NTC Contemporary Publishing Company, 1994.

Travis-Bildahl, Sandra. *A Day in the Life of a Midshipman.* Annapolis, MD: Naval Institute Press, 1996.

Van Orden, M. D. *U.S. Navy Ships and Coast Guard Cutters.* Annapolis, MD: Naval Institute Press, 2000.

RESOURCES

WEB SITE

U.S. MERCHANT MARINE ACADEMY

http://www.usmma.edu
This is the home page of the Merchant Marine Academy. It is has information about daily life, application procedures, classroom opportunities, and much more.

RESOURCES

WEB SITE

http://www.usmmaaa.com
This Web site gives details of life at the
academy and provides information on what
graduates do with their degrees.

INDEX

INDEX

ABOUT THE AUTHOR

Magdalena Alagna is an editor and a freelance writer who lives in New York City.